Not a
Ninja

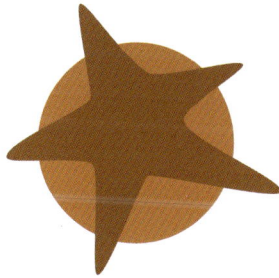

'Not a Ninja'
An original concept by Jenny Jinks
© Jenny Jinks 2022

Illustrated by Nathalia Rivera

Published by MAVERICK ARTS PUBLISHING LTD
Studio 11, City Business Centre, 6 Brighton Road,
Horsham, West Sussex, RH13 5BB
© Maverick Arts Publishing Limited May 2022
+44 (0)1403 256941

A CIP catalogue record for this book is available at the British Library.

ISBN 978-1-84886-884-7

Mave
publish
www.maverickb

Brown

This book is rated as: Brown Band (Guided Reading)

Not a Ninja

Written by
Jenny Jinks

Illustrated by
Nathalia Rivera

Chapter 1

"What am I going to do?" sighed the chief ninja. His voice echoed around the empty halls at Ninja HQ.

Not one ninja had turned up to his weekly briefing. Ninjas had been mysteriously disappearing for weeks, and now he had none left. And to make matters worse, he didn't have the first clue what had happened to them.

Sirens blared in the distance. Crime was sweeping the city streets. And without his ninjas there, secretly keeping the world safe, who would fix it?

He needed a new team. A better team. One that could find his ninjas and save the city. But where was he going to find them?

"Doddington!" the chief called. A short man rushed in and bowed low. "I have an important job for you. I need you to find me some new ninjas. Search far and wide. They need to be fast. They need to be clever. They need to be stealthy. I want nothing but the best!"

Chapter 2

Alex walked slowly out of the cafe, trying not to drop his hot chocolate, two doughnuts and a sandwich.

"Sorry!" he said, as he almost knocked over an old lady coming through the door.

"Whoa!" he said as the door bumped shut on him.

"Nooooooooooooooo!" he cried as his foot landed on something wobbly. Someone had left a skateboard outside the café. It started to roll, and took Alex with it. Somehow Alex was managing to keep his balance whilst dodging around all the people on the busy pavement and keep hold of his lunch. He was doing it! But the skateboard was going too fast, picking up speed as it whizzed downhill, straight towards... the main road! Where were the brakes?!

He heard someone yell, "Stop him!" But Alex couldn't stop. All he could do was...

JUMP!

Alex dived off the skateboard just in time.

Luckily, Alex had a soft landing. Not so lucky for the man he landed on though.

"Get off!" the man said crossly, shoving Alex to one side. Alex hurriedly got to his feet to help the man up, but his foot slipped on his doughnut.

His feet flew out from under him and he landed in a heap, right back on top of the man. Then something large and sloppy fell from the sky. It landed right on top of the man's head with an almighty

SPLAT!

Egg dripped down the man's red, angry face.

"Don't let him get away!" came a shout as police rushed towards them.

Oh no, I'm in big trouble now... thought Alex.

But it wasn't Alex that the police grabbed hold of. It was the man. They pulled him to his feet, and money spilled out of his pockets.

"Good lad," said a police officer, helping Alex off the floor and shaking his hand. "This man's a thief. He's been stealing from every shop in town. You're a hero, tackling him to the ground like that."

Alex shook his head. He was no hero, he was just clumsy. He went to take a sip of his hot chocolate—somehow he hadn't dropped it in all the commotion—when he noticed a note stuck to it.

An invitation.

How had that got there?

Chapter 3

Alex read the invitation again as he walked nervously up the huge, stone steps.

Congratulations, you have been chosen. Please join us at 2pm on Saturday.

Luckily there was a map showing where to go. Alex looked up at the enormous, fancy building.

"What is this place?" Alex whispered.

Bleep, bleep, blop.

"According to my research, this place doesn't even exist," a voice said behind him.

Alex spun round, tripping up the steps. A girl was behind him, tapping away on a device. "Which means this must be something ultra cool!" she added.

"I'm Alex," Alex said as they walked up the steps together. "Did you get a mysterious invitation too?"

"Bella," the girl said. "Yeah, a message popped up on my phone. Super mysterious. I guess we'll find out soon enough."

And they walked in through the giant double doors.

★★★

"Welcome, new recruits!" a deep voice boomed around the enormous hall.

A very short, elderly man had appeared in front of the small group of people.

"Let's get straight down to business," the man said. "You have all been chosen for your unique talents. I am sure you will all make me proud. So without further ado, let the training begin!"

A hand shot up from the group.

"Excuse me, but training for what?" the boy asked.

"Why, the reason you're all here, of course," the elderly man said, as if it was obvious. "You are going to be my new ninjas!"

Chapter 4

Alex was sure there must be some mistake. He couldn't be a ninja. Ninjas were smart and speedy and stealthy. And Alex was... well, the complete opposite.

And once the training began, Alex was even more sure. He had already got tangled in the ropes on the climbing challenge, and had only just managed to catch himself when he slipped off the high wire. He was useless.

"Maybe I should just quit," he muttered to himself.

"You can't quit," said Bella. "Just give it a try. It's easy."

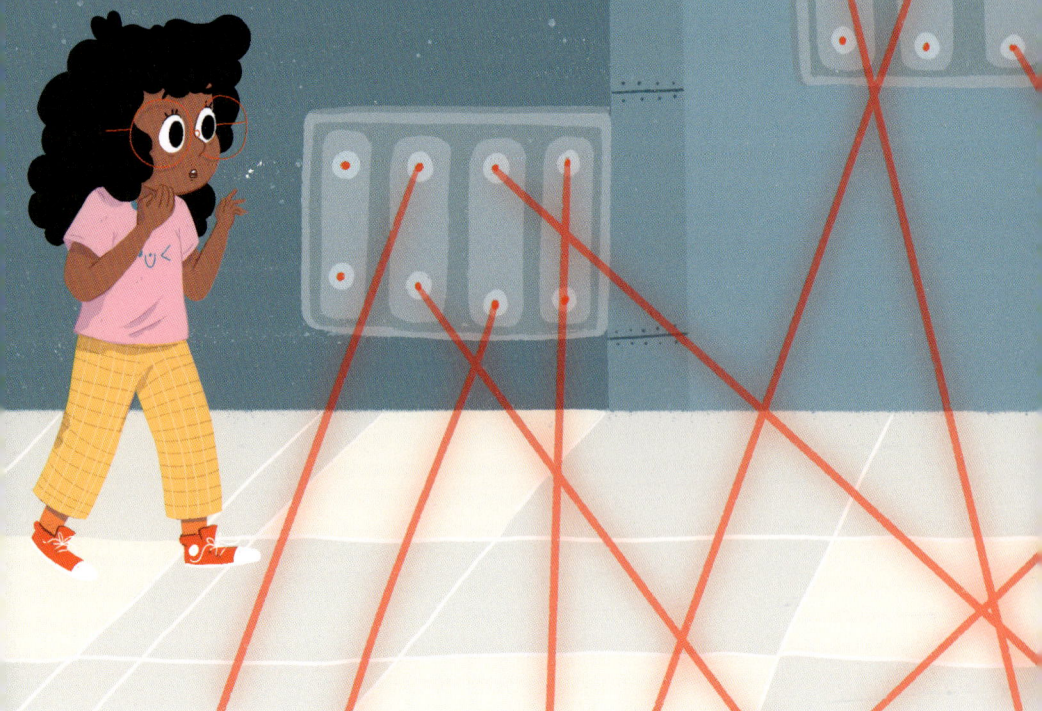

Alex looked at the next challenge—a room full of lasers. How was he supposed to get across that with his long, gangly legs? It was impossible.

Alex stepped over the first laser. So far so good. He crouched, rolled and slid past the next few. Maybe he could do it after all! But then his long legs got in a tangle. He stood on his laces. Before he knew it,

he had dived straight through the next few lasers, skidded across the room, and crashed headfirst into the wall on the other side. Alarms blared. Lights flashed. Alex's cheeks were burning.

"Hmmmm." The chief ninja frowned. He whispered something to Doddington, who hurriedly wrote on his clipboard. Alex was sure that was not a good sign.

"Next!"

Alex got to his feet to watch Bella, but she was too busy playing on her phone.

"Next!" The chief shouted more loudly.

"Bella!" Alex hissed.

Bleep, bleep, blop, went Bella's phone. All the lasers turned off, and Bella walked easily across the room.

"How did you do that?" Alex asked in astonishment.

"Like I said, it's easy when you know how," Bella grinned. "I just hacked the laser and switched it off!"

"You could have done that for me," Alex muttered to himself.

The rest of the training went much the same, and Alex wasn't the only one having trouble. Alex's long legs gave him a good head start in the speed test... but when he spotted one of the other recruits stopping for a rest, Alex just had to go back and help him. Bella, who had wheels in her shoes, whizzed past into first place.

Then, in the concealment round, everyone had to stay hidden. But another recruit knocked down a shelf, breaking the chief's favourite vase. The chief wasn't very impressed.

So when they were all called for a meeting, Alex was sure they were going to get fired. But instead, they were being sent on their first mission.

"Mission?!" everyone murmured with a mixture of excitement and fear.

"My ninjas are missing. Gone without a trace. But somebody *must* know something. Your job is to go out into the city and find out what you can. We must find them!"

Chapter 5

Alex felt a hint of excitement. A fact-finding mission. That didn't sound too dangerous. How much trouble could he get into?!

"Leave it to me," Bella said. She was already tapping away at her phone. "You can find out anything online. I'll have the information ultra fast. Why don't we get a drink while we wait?"

"This is the kind of mission I could get used to," said Boris, the slow recruit who had needed a rest in the speed test. He always seemed to need a rest.

"This isn't right," Alex said. "We're ninjas. We shouldn't be sitting around in a café! We should be out there looking for information. The chief is counting on us."

"I can do it!" said Bella, looking annoyed. "Trust me!"

Everyone else was quite happy doing things Bella's way. But Alex wasn't.

"Fine, I'll go on my own," Alex said, and he left.

But, now that he was all alone out on the streets, he had no idea where to start. What do you do when someone is missing?

Then Alex spotted a poster on a lamppost.

"Of course!" Alex said. "I'll put up missing posters!"

Alex spent the rest of the day printing posters of the missing ninjas and plastering them all over town. There wasn't one street corner or shop window that didn't have a poster in. Someone was sure to phone in with information any time now.

Chapter 6

When Alex got called back to Ninja HQ later, the others were already inside.

"What have you done?" roared the chief. "You are supposed to be ninjas! Ninjas are stealthy! Ninjas are secret! Ninjas do not sit around in coffee shops discussing secret matters in public!"

Alex saw the others all look down at their feet. He couldn't help but feel a little bit smug.

"And ninjas certainly don't put up posters! Now the whole world and his pet hamster knows about us!"

Everyone turned to look at Alex. Suddenly he didn't feel so smug. If the chief hadn't fired them before now, he certainly would now.

"You have left me no choice," the chief continued.

Here it comes, thought Alex.

"I'm going to have to…"

The chief was interrupted by Doddington rushing into the room. He whispered something to the chief. The chief cleared his throat.

"…send you on another mission," the chief continued. "Thanks to your posters we have just received a top tip-off. A lead at last!" The chief was actually smiling. "Go and get yourselves ready. Your next mission starts at sundown!"

Chapter 7

"That was close. I thought for sure we were going to get sacked!" Bella whispered to Alex as the ninjas set off for their mission. "Luckily, your mega plan saved us all."

"I don't know about that," Alex muttered. Didn't she realise that his stupid poster idea had almost got them sacked? He was just lucky that someone had seen one and phoned in when they did, telling them exactly where the ninjas were being held.

"Are we nearly there yet?" huffed Boris. "I need a break."

"We've barely started!" Bella laughed. She tapped on her phone. "According to my coordinates, the place is just up this hill."

They made the long, steep climb until they could see a large mansion above them.

"That must be the bad guy's lair," Boris said, finally catching up. "That's where they'll be holding the ninjas."

"Don't you think it's a bit odd that someone phoned in and told us exactly where the ninjas are?" Alex said. "What if it's a trap?"

"A trap?" Bella laughed. "There's no way the bad guys would be able to outsmart the chief like that."

But Alex wasn't so sure.

"Okay, but let's keep together. Remember what the chief said," Alex whispered as they gathered by the wall of the house. "We are just here for a fact-finding mission. We find the ninjas, check out the security and leave. That's it."

"Okay," everyone agreed. They all wanted to get it right this time and show the chief that they could do it.

"Bella, can you hack into the security system?" Alex began.

Bleep, bleep, blop.

"Already done!" Bella said proudly. "There's way more security around the back. I bet that's where they are holding the ninjas."

"I guess we can go now then," said Boris, turning back down the hill.

"What? No way! We need to get inside and check that the ninjas are really there!" Bella said.

"What if we get caught?" Alex said. Going inside wasn't part of the mission.

"I can unlock those doors. Then one of us can sneak inside and scout around. We'll be back out again in no time," Bella said.

"I'll go. Nobody ever notices me anyway," said a quiet voice. Everyone spun round. A small girl was

standing at the back of the group. Alex wasn't sure he had ever seen her before, but she was wearing a ninja suit just like them. The others seemed just as surprised.

"Great!" Bella beamed. "Then, uh..."

"Millie," said the girl. "But people call me Mouse."

"Mouse, you come with me," Bella said. "Alex, you stay here. We need someone to keep a lookout."

Before Alex had a chance to protest, Bella had told everyone where to go and they had all split up.

Alex didn't like this. He didn't like it one bit.

Chapter 8

It wasn't long before Alex heard footsteps and voices. *Phew*, he thought. They were back already.

But the footsteps were too heavy. And the voices were wrong.

Someone was coming.

Alex looked about for somewhere to hide, but there was nowhere. He was going to get caught!

What would a ninja do? He asked himself.

Then he spotted a drainpipe. It might be a stupid idea, but it was the only one he had.

He tried to focus only on the drainpipe as he climbed quickly and quietly up it. He made it onto the roof just as two guards came round the corner.

"Nobody here," one guard said to the other. And they walked away.

Yes! thought Alex triumphantly. Maybe he could be a ninja after all!

But where were the others? Surely they should be back by now.

Alex decided to have a look around. Light was coming through an open window upstairs. He scrabbled silently across the roof, terrified that he might fall at any moment. But somehow, he didn't. Finally, he was close enough to the window to hear voices inside.

"Where are they all now?" said a voice.

"Don't worry, they walked right into our trap," said a second voice.

Trap? thought Alex. *I knew it!*

"They've all been captured. All except one. But don't worry about him, he's useless."

Alex recognised that voice. He sneaked closer to the edge of the roof.

"Good work," the first voice said. "We couldn't have done it if you hadn't infiltrated them."

Infiltrated? Alex had to find out who was behind this. He held on to the gutter and dangled precariously over the edge. But he still wasn't low enough to see inside.

Then Alex heard a familiar sound.

Bleep, bleep, blop.

Everything happened at once. Alex's hands slipped. A roof tile slid. The gutter cracked. Alex fell off the roof. Swinging on the gutter, Alex smashed through the window and crashed right onto the table in the middle of the room.

Everyone froze. Alex froze.

And then a familiar face loomed over him.

Chapter 9

"Bella!" Alex cried, sitting up. "You're behind this!"

"I'm not surprised none of you figured it out. You're the worst bunch of ninjas I've ever seen. Barely even worth capturing," Bella said. "But after going to all that trouble of getting rid of the original ninjas, we couldn't have a new bunch taking over. So I pretended to be one of you. I gained your trust, and led you all right here."

"But... why?" Alex asked.

"Why?" Bella laughed. "All my life I've been desperate to join the ninjas. But the chief kept turning me away. I wasn't strong enough, or fast enough. Apparently it doesn't matter how smart you are. Smart people aren't heroes. That's not the ninja way. Well, I just had to show him exactly what smart people can do. And look, you all walked right into my trap—voluntarily! I've outsmarted all of you. Even the great chief himself. GUARDS! Take him!"

Alex had almost forgotten that the room was full of bad guys.

"But Bella, you made it! You're a ninja now. You don't need to do this," Alex pleaded, as the guards began to close in on him.

"You really think the chief is going to keep any of you on after all this?" Bella laughed a nasty, hollow laugh as the guards rushed round her towards Alex. "You might as well give up."

But Alex couldn't give up. He couldn't let his friends down. Filled with determination, he pushed himself up onto his hands and knees. Just then, he slid on the polished table and knocked all the cups flying at the oncoming guards. Boiling hot tea gushed towards them.

While the guards were distracted, Alex jumped off the table, sending it flipping backwards and knocking all the bad guys over.

As the alarm was raised through the building, more and more guards came rushing in. But they were in such a hurry to get to Alex that they got wedged in the door and fell in a heap. Alex was taking the opportunity to look for a way out, when he thought he saw a familiar little head in a black suit creep in through the door.

And then everything went black.

When the lights came back on, everyone was tied up and sirens wailed up the hill towards them.

And Alex was gone.

Chapter 10

Where AM I? thought Alex.

One minute he was hiding in a room full of angry guards and bad guys. The next minute, everything went black, and he was being pulled out of the window into the cold night air.

All the ninjas, old and new, were on the roof top.

"Follow me," whispered one of the original ninjas, and they slid silently down the drainpipe and slipped away into the night.

Back at Ninja HQ, everyone crowded around Alex.

"You saved us!"

"You were so brave!"

"Did you really take down all the bad guys and guards on your own?"

They clapped Alex on the back and shook his hand like he was a hero.

"I don't understand," said Alex. "What just happened?"

"Thanks to you causing a huge distraction and

taking down all the guards, we were able to escape," said Boris. "Then we found the others and set them free."

"Yeah! You should have seen Boris break down the door!" Mouse squeaked excitedly. Then she blushed bright red.

"Then, while the other ninjas went to turn the lights out, Mouse snuck into the room and was tying people up before they even knew what was happening! She was amazing!" Boris grinned. Mouse blushed even harder and looked at her feet, clearly wishing everyone would go back to not noticing her again. "Then we grabbed you and got out!"

"Wow, well done everyone," Alex said.

"We couldn't have done any of it without you," Mouse said quietly.

Alex looked around at everyone. This might be the last time they were all together. Like Bella had said, the chief wouldn't keep them now the original ninjas were back. Alex was surprised at how sad he felt.

★ ★ ★

"Let me get this straight," the chief said, still in his pyjamas and stifling a yawn. "You ignored every single one of my orders."

The ninjas shuffled their feet awkwardly.

"And, in one night, with absolutely no experience, you broke into enemy headquarters, found the captured ninjas, freed them, captured all of the bad guys and discovered an imposter among us."

The chief paused and shook his head.

"I have never been more proud of a bunch of new recruits."

Alex looked up in disbelief.

"You might be nothing like my previous teams, but maybe it's about time we did things a little differently round here. If you want to stay, of course."

Alex looked at the others and they all grinned. Of course he was staying. He was part of a team. He was finally a ninja!

Discussion Points

1. Why does the chief ninja need more ninjas?

2. How does Alex catch the thief in the beginning?
a) He gives him his egg sandwich
b) He uses some rope
c) He accidently lands on him

3. What was your favourite part of the story?

4. Who infiltrated the ninjas?

5. Why do you think Alex didn't want the team to split up?

6. Who was your favourite character and why?

7. There were moments in the story when Alex **tried his best**. Where do you think the story shows this most?

8. What do you think happens after the end of the story?

Book Bands for Guided Reading

The Institute of Education book banding system is a scale of colours that reflects the various levels of reading difficulty. The bands are assigned by taking into account the content, the language style, the layout and phonics. Word, phrase and sentence level work is also taken into consideration.

The Maverick Readers Scheme is a bright, attractive range of books covering the pink to grey bands. All of these books have been book banded for guided reading to the industry standard and edited by a leading educational consultant.

To view the whole Maverick Readers scheme, visit our website at

www.maverickearlyreaders.com

Or scan the QR code to view our scheme instantly!

Maverick Chapter Readers
(From Lime to Grey Band)

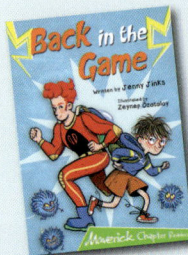

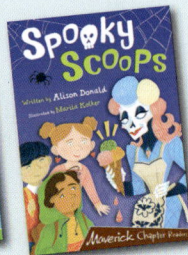

Back in the Game
Written by Jonny Zinks

Spooky Scoops
Written by Alison Donald

Secret Spaniel